UNDER MILK WOOD

By Dylan Thomas

COLLECTED POEMS, 1934–1952

DEATHS AND ENTRANCES
  Poems

PORTRAIT OF THE ARTIST AS A
                    YOUNG DOG
  Fictional autobiography

UNDER MILK WOOD
  A play for voices

THE DOCTOR AND THE DEVILS
  A film scenario

QUITE EARLY ONE MORNING
  Broadcasts

A PROSPECT OF THE SEA
  Stories and prose writings

LETTERS TO VERNON WATKINS

DYLAN THOMAS

☆

Under Milk Wood

A Play for Voices

Preface and musical settings by
DANIEL JONES

LONDON
J. M. DENT & SONS LTD

PREFACE

On the 9th of November 1953, a few days after his thirty-ninth birthday, Dylan Thomas died in New York. At the time of his death a new poem was still unfinished, and the collaboration with Stravinsky, planned for the end of the year, had not even begun. The survival of *Under Milk Wood* is a remarkable piece of good fortune, for it was not completed until Thomas came within a month of his death, though he had worked intermittently on the play for nearly ten years. There was no time for any final revision of the text by the poet himself, but we are justified in regarding what he has left as a complete work.

The publication of Thomas's *Collected Poems* in 1952 marked the end of one period of his literary development; after this, according to his own words, he intended to turn from the strictly personal kind of poetry to a more public form of expression, and to large-scale dramatic works in particular, where there would be scope for all his versatility, for his gifts of humour and characterization as well as his genius for poetry. It is fortunate that at least one of these projected works has been preserved for us.

Under Milk Wood, a Play for Voices grew by a slow and natural process, and the story of that growth, known only to a few friends of the poet, is most interesting. Thomas liked small towns by the sea best, and small Welsh towns by the sea best of all. Before the war he lived for many years in Laugharne, and during the war for a time in New Quay; there is no doubt that he absorbed the spirit of these places and, through imagination and insight, the spirit of all other places like them. When, more than ten years ago, a short talk was commissioned by the B.B.C., the description of a small Welsh seaside town was a natural choice of subject. *Quite Early One Morning*, short as it is, and written so many years ago, is closely related to *Under Milk Wood*. There is the same sequence of time, though limited to the morning hours and in winter, not spring; we hear the dreams of the sleeping town and see the sleepers getting up and going about their business. Captain Tiny Evans and the Rev. Thomas Evans are pygmies beside the blind sea-captain and the reverend bard of Llaregyb, but Miss Hughes 'The Cosy' recalls Myfanwy Price, Manchester House stands ready for Mog Edwards, and the husbands of Mrs Ogmore-Pritchard are already at their tasks: 'Dust the china, feed the canary, sweep the drawing-room floor; and before you let the sun in, mind he wipes his shoes.'

The success of this broadcast talk suggested to Thomas a more extended work against the same kind of background. At first he was unable to decide upon the form of the work, and there was much discussion with friends about a stage play, a comedy in verse, and a radio play with a blind man as narrator and central character. The blind man, a natural bridge between eye and ear for the radio listener, survives in *Under Milk Wood*, with the difference that Captain Cat is made to share his central position with two anonymous narrators. But the simple time sequence of *Quite Early One Morning*, which resembles the pattern of *Under Milk Wood* so closely, at first appeared inadequate; some kind of plot seemed to be necessary. Thomas thought he had found the theme he wanted in the contrast between the mythical town and the surrounding world, the conflict between the eccentrics, strong in their individuality and freedom, and the sane ones who sacrifice everything to some notion of conformity. The whole population cannot very well be accommodated inside the walls of a lunatic asylum; so the sane world decrees that the town itself shall be declared an 'insane area,' with all traffic and goods diverted from it. Captain Cat, spokesman of the indignant citizens, insists that the sanity of the town should be put on trial in the town hall with every legal formality; he will be Counsel for the Defence and the citizens themselves will be witnesses. The trial takes place, but it comes to a surprising end. The final speech for the Prosecution consists of a full and minute description of the ideally sane town; as soon as they hear this, the people withdraw their defence and beg to be cordoned off from the sane world as soon as possible.

Once more settled in his house overlooking Laugharne Estuary, Thomas began working according to the plan of *The Town Was Mad*, as he called it, and brought the action up to the delivery of letters by Willy Nilly the postman; but by that time he had changed his mind, and there was no letter for Captain Cat about the sanity or the insanity of the town. When this first part of *Under Milk Wood*, with the provisional title *Llaregyb, a Piece for Radio Perhaps*, appeared for the first time in *Betteghe Oscure*,[1] Thomas had returned to the plan of *Quite Early One Morning*; his intention was to limit the picture to the town itself, with hardly a suggestion of a world beyond the town, and to extend the time sequence to form a complete cycle.

[1] *Quaderno IX*, edited by Marguerite Caetani (Rome, 1952).

Before Thomas's third visit to the U.S.A. in 1953, the title *Under Milk Wood, a Play for Voices* was decided upon, the first part, *Llaregyb*, was revised, and the work had been extended to the end of Polly Garter's song, where it first appears. In this form the play was read at the Kaufmann Auditorium of the Young Men's Hebrew Association on the 15th and the 29th of May; the poet himself read the parts of the First Voice and the Rev. Eli Jenkins.

As soon as Thomas returned to Britain the B.B.C. urged him to complete the work without further delay, and, by omitting some projected ballads and unfinished material for the closing section, he was able to supply a finished version at the end of October. The first broadcast of the whole work, produced by Douglas Cleverdon with a distinguished all Welsh cast, was given on the 25th of January 1954, with a repetition two days later.

In case *Under Milk Wood* falls into the hands of a Welsh philologist, it must be made clear that the language used is Anglo-Welsh. Dylan Thomas spoke no Welsh, and the reader must imitate his inconsistency if he wishes to hear the words as they were pronounced by the poet himself. A note on pronunciation will be found at the end of the text.

DANIEL JONES.

January 1954.

CONTENTS

ix

UNDER MILK WOOD

[*Silence*]

FIRST VOICE (*Very softly*)

To begin at the beginning:

It is spring, moonless night in the small town, starless and bible-black, the cobblestreets silent and the hunched, courters'-and-rabbits' wood limping invisible down to the sloeblack, slow, black, crowblack, fishingboat-bobbing sea. The houses are blind as moles (though moles see fine to-night in the snouting, velvet dingles) or blind as Captain Cat there in the muffled middle by the pump and the town clock, the shops in mourning, the Welfare Hall in widows' weeds. And all the people of the lulled and dumbfound town are sleeping now.

Hush, the babies are sleeping, the farmers, the fishers, the tradesmen and pensioners, cobbler, school-teacher, postman and publican, the undertaker and the fancy woman, drunkard, dressmaker, preacher, police-man, the webfoot cocklewomen and the tidy wives. Young girls lie bedded soft or glide in their dreams, with rings and trousseaux, bridesmaided by glow-worms down the aisles of the organplaying wood. The boys are dreaming wicked or of the bucking ranches of the night and the jollyrodgered sea. And the anthracite statues of the horses sleep in the fields, and

1

the cows in the byres, and the dogs in the wetnosed yards; and the cats nap in the slant corners or lope sly, streaking and needling, on the one cloud of the roofs.

You can hear the dew falling, and the hushed town breathing. Only *your* eyes are unclosed to see the black and folded town fast, and slow, asleep. And you alone can hear the invisible starfall, the darkest-before-dawn minutely dewgrazed stir of the black, dab-filled sea where the *Arethusa*, the *Curlew* and the *Skylark*, *Zanzibar*, *Rhiannon*, the *Rover*, the *Cormorant*, and the *Star of Wales* tilt and ride.

Listen. It is night moving in the streets, the processional salt slow musical wind in Coronation Street and Cockle Row, it is the grass growing on Llaregyb Hill, dewfall, starfall, the sleep of birds in Milk Wood.

Listen. It is night in the chill, squat chapel, hymning in bonnet and brooch and bombazine black, butterfly choker and bootlace bow, coughing like nannygoats, sucking mintoes, fortywinking hallelujah; night in the four-ale, quiet as a domino; in Ocky Milkman's lofts like a mouse with gloves; in Dai Bread's bakery flying like black flour. It is to-night in Donkey Street, trotting silent, with seaweed on its hooves, along the cockled cobbles, past curtained fernpot, text and trinket, harmonium, holy dresser, watercolours done by hand, china dog and rosy tin teacaddy. It is night neddying among the snuggeries of babies.

Look. It is night, dumbly, royally winding through the Coronation cherry trees; going through the graveyard of Bethesda with winds gloved and folded, and dew doffed; tumbling by the Sailors Arms.

Time passes. Listen. Time passes.

Come closer now.

Only you can hear the houses sleeping in the streets in the slow deep salt and silent black, bandaged night. Only you can see, in the blinded bedrooms, the combs and petticoats over the chairs, the jugs and basins, the glasses of teeth, Thou Shalt Not on the wall, and the yellowing dickybird-watching pictures of the dead. Only you can hear and see, behind the eyes of the sleepers, the movements and countries and mazes and colours and dismays and rainbows and tunes and wishes and flight and fall and despairs and big seas of their dreams.

From where you are, you can hear their dreams.

Captain Cat, the retired blind seacaptain, asleep in his bunk in the seashelled, ship-in-bottled, shipshape best cabin of Schooner House dreams of

SECOND VOICE

never such seas as any that swamped the decks of his S.S. *Kidwelly* bellying over the bedclothes and jellyfish-slippery sucking him down salt deep into the Davy dark where the fish come biting out and nibble him down to his wishbone, and the long drowned nuzzle up to him.

FIRST DROWNED

Remember me, Captain?

CAPTAIN CAT

You're Dancing Williams!

FIRST DROWNED

I lost my step in Nantucket.

SECOND DROWNED

Do you see me, Captain? the white bone talking? I'm Tom-Fred the donkeyman . . . we shared the same girl once . . . her name was Mrs Probert . . .

WOMAN'S VOICE

Rosie Probert, thirty three Duck Lane. Come on up, boys, I'm dead.

THIRD DROWNED

Hold me, Captain, I'm Jonah Jarvis, come to a bad end, very enjoyable.

FOURTH DROWNED

Alfred Pomeroy Jones, sea-lawyer, born in Mumbles, sung like a linnet, crowned you with a flagon, tattooed with mermaids, thirst like a dredger, died of blisters.

FIRST DROWNED

This skull at your earhole is

FIFTH DROWNED

Curly Bevan. Tell my auntie it was me that pawned the ormolu clock.

CAPTAIN CAT

Aye, aye, Curly.

SECOND DROWNED

Tell my missus no I never

THIRD DROWNED

I never done what she said I never.

FOURTH DROWNED

Yes they did.

FIFTH DROWNED

And who brings coconuts and shawls and parrots
to *my* Gwen now?

FIRST DROWNED

How's it above?

SECOND DROWNED

Is there rum and laverbread?

THIRD DROWNED

Bosoms and robins?

FOURTH DROWNED

Concertinas?

FIFTH DROWNED

Ebenezer's bell?

FIRST DROWNED

Fighting and onions?

SECOND DROWNED

And sparrows and daisies?

THIRD DROWNED

Tiddlers in a jamjar?

FOURTH DROWNED

Buttermilk and whippets?

FIFTH DROWNED

Rock-a-bye baby?

FIRST DROWNED

Washing on the line?

SECOND DROWNED

And old girls in the snug?

THIRD DROWNED

How's the tenors in Dowlais?

FOURTH DROWNED

Who milks the cows in Maesgwyn?

FIFTH DROWNED

When she smiles, is there dimples?

FIRST DROWNED

What's the smell of parsley?

CAPTAIN CAT

Oh, my dead dears!

FIRST VOICE

From where you are you can hear in Cockle Row in the spring, moonless night, Miss Price, dressmaker and sweetshop-keeper, dream of

SECOND VOICE

her lover, tall as the town clock tower, Samson-syrup-gold-maned, whacking thighed and piping hot, thunderbolt-bass'd and barnacle-breasted, flailing up the cockles with his eyes like blowlamps and scooping low over her lonely loving hotwaterbottled body.

MR EDWARDS

Myfanwy Price!

MISS PRICE

Mr Mog Edwards!

MR EDWARDS

I am a draper mad with love. I love you more than all the flannelette and calico, candlewick, dimity, crash and merino, tussore, cretonne, crepon, muslin, poplin, ticking and twill in the whole Cloth Hall of the

6

world. I have come to take you away to my Emporium on the hill, where the change hums on wires. Throw away your little bedsocks and your Welsh wool knitted jacket, I will warm the sheets like an electric toaster, I will lie by your side like the Sunday roast.

MISS PRICE

I will knit you a wallet of forget-me-not blue, for the money to be comfy. I will warm your heart by the fire so that you can slip it in under your vest when the shop is closed.

MR EDWARDS

Myfanwy, Myfanwy, before the mice gnaw at your bottom drawer will you say

MISS PRICE

Yes, Mog, yes, Mog, yes, yes, yes.

MR EDWARDS

And all the bells of the tills of the town shall ring for our wedding. [*Noise of money-tills and chapel bells*

FIRST VOICE

Come now, drift up the dark, come up the drifting sea-dark street now in the dark night seesawing like the sea, to the bible-black airless attic over Jack Black the cobbler's shop where alone and savagely Jack Black sleeps in a nightshirt tied to his ankles with elastic and dreams of

SECOND VOICE

chasing the naughty couples down the grassgreen gooseberried double bed of the wood, flogging the tosspots in the spit-and-sawdust, driving out the bare bold girls from the sixpenny hops of his nightmares.

JACK BLACK (*Loudly*)
Ach y fi!
Ach y fi!

Evans the Death, the undertaker,

laughs high and aloud in his sleep and curls up his toes
as he sees, upon waking fifty years ago, snow lie deep on
the goosefield behind the sleeping house; and he runs
out into the field where his mother is making welshcakes in the snow, and steals a fistful of snowflakes and
currants and climbs back to bed to eat them cold and
sweet under the warm, white clothes while his mother
dances in the snow kitchen crying out for her lost
currants.

And in the little pink-eyed cottage next to the undertaker's, lie, alone, the seventeen snoring gentle stone
of Mister Waldo, rabbitcatcher, barber, herbalist,
catdoctor, quack, his fat pink hands, palms up, over
the edge of the patchwork quilt, his black boots neat
and tidy in the washing-basin, his bowler on a nail
above the bed, a milk stout and a slice of cold bread
pudding under the pillow; and, dripping in the dark,
he dreams of

This little piggy went to market
This little piggy stayed at home
This little piggy had roast beef
This little piggy had none
And this little piggy went

8

LITTLE BOY
wee wee wee wee wee

MOTHER
all the way home to

WIFE (*Screaming*)
Waldo!   Wal-do!

MR WALDO
Yes, Blodwen love?

WIFE
Oh, what'll the neighbours say, what'll the neighbours . . .

FIRST NEIGHBOUR
Poor Mrs Waldo

SECOND NEIGHBOUR
What she puts up with

FIRST NEIGHBOUR
Never should of married

SECOND NEIGHBOUR
If she didn't had to

FIRST NEIGHBOUR
Same as her mother

SECOND NEIGHBOUR
There's a husband for you

FIRST NEIGHBOUR
Bad as his father

SECOND NEIGHBOUR

And you know where he ended

FIRST NEIGHBOUR

Up in the asylum

SECOND NEIGHBOUR

Crying for his ma

FIRST NEIGHBOUR

Every Saturday

SECOND NEIGHBOUR

He hasn't got a log

FIRST NEIGHBOUR

And carrying on

SECOND NEIGHBOUR

With that Mrs Beattie Morris

FIRST NEIGHBOUR

Up in the quarry

SECOND NEIGHBOUR

And seen her baby

FIRST NEIGHBOUR

It's got his nose

SECOND NEIGHBOUR

Oh it makes my heart bleed

FIRST NEIGHBOUR

What he'll do for drink

SECOND NEIGHBOUR

He sold the pianola

FIRST NEIGHBOUR

And her sewing machine

SECOND NEIGHBOUR

Falling in the gutter

FIRST NEIGHBOUR

Talking to the lamp-post

SECOND NEIGHBOUR

Using language

FIRST NEIGHBOUR

Singing in the w

SECOND NEIGHBOUR

Poor Mrs Waldo

WIFE (*Tearfully*)

. . . Oh, Waldo, Waldo!

MR WALDO

Hush, love, hush. I'm *widower* Waldo now.

MOTHER (*Screaming*)

Waldo, Wal-do!

LITTLE BOY

Yes, our mum?

MOTHER

Oh, what'll the neighbours say, what'll the neighbours . . .

THIRD NEIGHBOUR

Black as a chimbley

FOURTH NEIGHBOUR

Ringing doorbells

THIRD NEIGHBOUR

Breaking windows

FOURTH NEIGHBOUR

Making mudpies

THIRD NEIGHBOUR

Stealing currants

FOURTH NEIGHBOUR

Chalking words

THIRD NEIGHBOUR

Saw him in the bushes

FOURTH NEIGHBOUR

Playing mwchins

THIRD NEIGHBOUR

Send him to bed without any supper

FOURTH NEIGHBOUR

Give him sennapods and lock him in the dark

THIRD NEIGHBOUR

Off to the reformatory

FOURTH NEIGHBOUR

Off to the reformatory

TOGETHER

Learn him with a slipper on his b.t.m.

ANOTHER MOTHER (*Screaming*)

Waldo, Wal-do! what you doing with our Matti?

LITTLE BOY

Give us a kiss, Matti Richards.

LITTLE GIRL

Give us a penny then.

MR WALDO

I only got a halfpenny.

FIRST WOMAN

Lips is a penny.

PREACHER

Will you take this woman Matti Richards

SECOND WOMAN

Dulcie Prothero

THIRD WOMAN

Effie Bevan

FOURTH WOMAN

Lil the Gluepot

FIFTH WOMAN

Mrs Flusher

WIFE

Blodwen Bowen

PREACHER

To be your awful wedded wife

LITTLE BOY (*Screaming*)

No, no, no!

Now, in her iceberg-white, holily laundered crino-
line nightgown, under virtuous polar sheets, in her
spruced and scoured dust-defying bedroom in trig and
trim Bay View, a house for paying guests, at the top
of the town, Mrs Ogmore-Pritchard widow, twice, of
Mr Ogmore, linoleum, retired, and Mr Pritchard,
failed bookmaker, who maddened by besoming, swab-
bing and scrubbing, the voice of the vacuum-cleaner
and the fume of polish, ironically swallowed dis-
infectant, fidgets in her rinsed sleep, wakes in a dream,
and nudges in the ribs dead Mr Ogmore, dead Mr
Pritchard, ghostly on either side.

MRS OGMORE-PRITCHARD
Mr Ogmore!
Mr Pritchard!
It is time to inhale your balsam.

MR OGMORE
Oh, Mrs Ogmore!

MR PRITCHARD
Oh, Mrs Pritchard!

MRS PRITCHARD
Soon it will be time to get up.
Tell me your tasks, in order.

MR OGMORE
I must put my pyjamas in the drawer marked pyjamas.

MR PRITCHARD
I must take my cold bath which is good for me.

MR OGMORE

I must wear my flannel band to ward off sciatica.

MR PRITCHARD

I must dress behind the curtain and put on my apron.

MR OGMORE

I must blow my nose.

MRS OGMORE-PRITCHARD

In the garden, if you please.

MR OGMORE

In a piece of tissue-paper which I afterwards burn.

MR PRITCHARD

I must take my salts which are nature's friend.

MR OGMORE

I must boil the drinking water because of germs.

MR PRITCHARD

I must make my herb tea which is free from tannin.

MR OGMORE

And have a charcoal biscuit which is good for me.

MR PRITCHARD

I may smoke one pipe of asthma mixture.

MRS OGMORE-PRITCHARD

In the woodshed, if you please.

MR PRITCHARD

And dust the parlour and spray the canary.

MR OGMORE

I must put on rubber gloves and search the peke for fleas.

MR PRITCHARD

I must dust the blinds and then I must raise them.

MRS OGMORE-PRITCHARD

And before you let the sun in, mind it wipes its shoes.

FIRST VOICE

In Butcher Beynon's, Gossamer Beynon, daughter, schoolteacher, dreaming deep, daintily ferrets under a fluttering hummock of chicken's feathers in a slaughter-house that has chintz curtains and a three-pieced suite, and finds, with no surprise, a small rough ready man with a bushy tail winking in a paper carrier.

GOSSAMER BEYNON

At last, my love,

FIRST VOICE

sighs Gossamer Beynon. And the bushy tail wags rude and ginger.

ORGAN MORGAN

Help,

SECOND VOICE

cries Organ Morgan, the organist, in his dream,

ORGAN MORGAN

There is perturbation and music in Coronation Street! All the spouses are honking like geese and the babies singing opera.   P.C. Attila Rees has got his truncheon out and is playing cadenzas by the pump, the cows from Sunday Meadow ring like reindeer, and on the roof of Handel Villa see the Women's Welfare hoofing, bloomered, in the moon.

FIRST VOICE

At the sea-end of town, Mr and Mrs Floyd, the cocklers, are sleeping as quiet as death, side by wrinkled side, toothless, salt and brown, like two old kippers in a box.

And high above, in Salt Lake Farm, Mr Utah Watkins counts, all night, the wife-faced sheep as they leap the fences on the hill, smiling and knitting and bleating just like Mrs Utah Watkins.

UTAH WATKINS (*Yawning*)

Thirty - four, thirty - five, thirty - six, forty - eight, eighty-nine . . .

MRS UTAH WATKINS (*Bleating*)
Knit one slip one
Knit two together
Pass the slipstitch over . . .

FIRST VOICE

Ocky Milkman, drowned asleep in Cockle Street, is emptying his churns into the Dewi River,

OCKY MILKMAN (*Whispering*)
regardless of expense,

FIRST VOICE

and weeping like a funeral.

17

Cherry Owen, next door, lifts a tankard to his lips but nothing flows out of it. He shakes the tankard. It turns into a fish. He drinks the fish.

FIRST VOICE

P.C. Attila Rees lumps out of bed, dead to the dark and still foghorning, and drags out his helmet from under the bed; but deep in the backyard lock-up of his sleep a mean voice murmurs

A VOICE (*Murmuring*)

You'll be sorry for this in the morning,

FIRST VOICE

and he heave-ho's back to bed. His helmet swashes in the dark.

SECOND VOICE

Willy Nilly, postman, asleep up street, walks four-teen miles to deliver the post as he does every day of the night, and rat-a-tats hard and sharp on Mrs Willy Nilly.

MRS WILLY NILLY

Don't spank me, please, teacher,

SECOND VOICE

whimpers his wife at his side, but every night of her married life she has been late for school.

FIRST VOICE

Sinbad Sailors, over the taproom of the Sailors Arms, hugs his damp pillow whose secret name is Gossamer Beynon.

A mogul catches Lily Smalls in the wash-house.

Ooh, you old mogul!

SECOND VOICE

Mrs Rose Cottage's eldest, Mae, peals off her pink-and-white skin in a furnace in a tower in a cave in a waterfall in a wood and waits there raw as an onion for Mister Right to leap up the burning tall hollow splashes of leaves like a brilliantined trout.

MAE ROSE COTTAGE (*Very close and softly, drawing out the words*)
                    Call me Dolores
                    Like they do in the stories.

FIRST VOICE

Alone until she dies, Bessie Bighead, hired help, born in the workhouse, smelling of the cowshed, snores bass and gruff on a couch of straw in a loft in Salt Lake Farm and picks a posy of daisies in Sunday Meadow to put on the grave of Gomer Owen who kissed her once by the pig-sty when she wasn't looking and never kissed her again although she was looking all the time.

And the Inspectors of Cruelty fly down into Mrs Butcher Beynon's dream to persecute Mr Beynon for selling

BUTCHER BEYNON

owlmeat, dogs' eyes, manchop.

SECOND VOICE

Mr Beynon, in butcher's bloodied apron, spring-heels down Coronation Street, a finger, not his own, in his mouth. Straightfaced in his cunning sleep he pulls the legs of his dreams and

BUTCHER BEYNON
hunting on pigback shoots down the wild giblets.

ORGAN MORGAN (*High and softly*)
Help!

GOSSAMER BEYNON (*Softly*)
My foxy darling.

FIRST VOICE
Now behind the eyes and secrets of the dreamers
in the streets rocked to sleep by the sea, see the

SECOND VOICE
titbits and topsyturvies, bobs and buttontops, bags
and bones, ash and rind and dandruff and nailparings,
saliva and snowflakes and moulted feathers of dreams,
the wrecks and sprats and shells and fishbones, whale-
juice and moonshine and small salt fry dished up by the
hidden sea.

FIRST VOICE
The owls are hunting. Look, over Bethesda grave-
stones one hoots and swoops and catches a mouse by
Hannah Rees, Beloved Wife. And in Coronation
Street, which you alone can see it is so dark under the
chapel in the skies, the Reverend Eli Jenkins, poet,
preacher, turns in his deep towards-dawn sleep and
dreams of

REV. ELI JENKINS
Eisteddfodau.

SECOND VOICE
He intricately rhymes, to the music of crwth and
pibgorn, all night long in his druid's seedy nightie in a
beer-tent black with parchs.

Mr Pugh, schoolmaster, fathoms asleep, pretends
to be sleeping, spies foxy round the droop of his night-
cap and pssst! whistles up

MR PUGH

Murder.

FIRST VOICE

Mrs Organ Morgan, groceress, coiled grey like a
dormouse, her paws to her ears, conjures

MRS ORGAN MORGAN

Silence.

SECOND VOICE

She sleeps very dulcet in a cove of wool, and trumpet-
ing Organ Morgan at her side snores no louder than a
spider.

FIRST VOICE

Mary Ann Sailors dreams of

MARY ANN SAILORS

The Garden of Eden.

FIRST VOICE

She comes in her smock-frock and clogs

MARY ANN SAILORS

away from the cool scrubbed cobbled kitchen with the
Sunday-school pictures on the whitewashed wall and
the farmers' almanac hung above the settle and the
sides of bacon on the ceiling hooks, and goes down the
cockleshelled paths of that applepie kitchen garden,
ducking under the gippo's clothespegs, catching her
apron on the blackcurrant bushes, past beanrows and
onion-bed and tomatoes ripening on the wall towards

the old man playing the harmonium in the orchard, and sits down on the grass at his side and shells the green peas that grow up through the lap of her frock that brushes the dew.

In Donkey Street, so furred with sleep, Dai Bread, Polly Garter, Nogood Boyo, and Lord Cut-Glass sigh before the dawn that is about to be and dream of

Harems.

Babies.

Nothing.

Tick tock tick tock tick tock tick tock.

Time passes. Listen. Time passes. An owl flies home past Bethesda, to a chapel in an oak. And the dawn inches up.

[*One distant bell-note, faintly reverberating*

Stand on this hill. This is Llaregyb Hill, old as the hills, high, cool, and green, and from this small circle of stones, made not by druids but by Mrs Beynon's Billy, you can see all the town below you sleeping in the first of the dawn.

You can hear the love-sick woodpigeons mooning in bed. A dog barks in his sleep, farmyards away. The town ripples like a lake in the waking haze.

22

Less than five hundred souls inhabit the three quaint streets and the few narrow by-lanes and scattered farmsteads that constitute this small, decaying watering-place which may, indeed, be called a 'backwater of life' without disrespect to its natives who possess, to this day, a salty individuality of their own. The main street, Coronation Street, consists, for the most part, of humble, two-storied houses many of which attempt to achieve some measure of gaiety by prinking themselves out in crude colours and by the liberal use of pinkwash, though there are remaining a few eighteenth-century houses of more pretension, if, on the whole, in a sad state of disrepair. Though there is little to attract the hillclimber, the healthseeker, the sportsman, or the weekending motorist, the contemplative may, if sufficiently attracted to spare it some leisurely hours, find, in its cobbled streets and its little fishing harbour, in its several curious customs, and in the conversation of its local 'characters,' some of that picturesque sense of the past so frequently lacking in towns and villages which have kept more abreast of the times. The River Dewi is said to abound in trout, but is much poached. The one place of worship, with its neglected graveyard, is of no architectural interest.

[A cock crows

FIRST VOICE

The principality of the sky lightens now, over our green hill, into spring morning larked and crowed and belling.

[Slow bell notes

Who pulls the townhall bellrope but blind Captain Cat? One by one, the sleepers are rung out of sleep this one morning as every morning. And soon you shall see the chimneys' slow upflying snow as Captain Cat, in sailor's cap and seaboots, announces to-day with his loud get-out-of-bed bell.

The Reverend Eli Jenkins, in Bethesda House, gropes out of bed into his preacher's black, combs back his bard's white hair, forgets to wash, pads barefoot downstairs, opens the front door, stands in the doorway and, looking out at the day and up at the eternal hill, and hearing the sea break and the gab of birds, remembers his own verses and tells them softly to empty Coronation Street that is rising and raising its blinds.

REV. ELI JENKINS

Dear Gwalia! I know there are
Towns lovelier than ours,
And fairer hills and loftier far,
And groves more full of flowers,

And boskier woods more blithe with spring
And bright with birds' adorning,
And sweeter bards than I to sing
Their praise this beauteous morning.

By Cader Idris, tempest-torn,
Or Moel yr Wyddfa's glory,
Carnedd Llewelyn beauty born,
Plinlimmon old in story,

By mountains where King Arthur dreams,
By Penmaenmawr defiant,
Llaregyb Hill a molehill seems,
A pygmy to a giant.

By Sawdde, Senny, Dovey, Dee,
Edw, Eden, Aled, all,
Taff and Towy broad and free,
Llyfnant with its waterfall,

Claerwen, Cleddau, Dulais, Daw,
Ely, Gwili, Ogwr, Nedd,
Small is our River Dewi, Lord,
A baby on a rushy bed.

By Carreg Cennen, King of time,
Our Heron Head is only
A bit of stone with seaweed spread
Where gulls come to be lonely.

A tiny dingle is Milk Wood
By Golden Grove 'neath Grongar,
But let me choose and oh! I should
Love all my life and longer

To stroll among our trees and stray
In Goosegog Lane, on Donkey Down,
And hear the Dewi sing all day,
And never, never leave the town.

SECOND VOICE

The Reverend Jenkins closes the front door. His
morning service is over.

[*Slow bell notes*

25

Now, woken at last by the out-of-bed-sleepy-head-
Polly-put-the-kettle-on townhall bell, Lily Smalls, Mrs
Beynon's treasure, comes downstairs from a dream
of royalty who all night long went larking with her
full of sauce in the Milk Wood dark, and puts the kettle
on the primus ring in Mrs Beynon's kitchen, and looks
at herself in Mr Beynon's shaving-glass over the sink,
and sees:

LILY SMALLS

Oh there's a face!
Where you get that hair from?
Got it from a old tom cat.
Give it back then, love.
Oh there's a perm!

Where you get that nose from, Lily?
Got it from my father, silly.
You've got it on upside down!
Oh there's a conk!

Look at your complexion!
Oh no, *you* look.
Needs a bit of make-up.
Needs a veil.
Oh there's glamour!

Where you get that smile, Lil?
Never you mind, girl.
Nobody loves you.
That's what *you* think.

Who is it loves you?
Shan't tell.
Come on, Lily.
Cross your heart then?
Cross my heart.

FIRST VOICE

And very softly, her lips almost touching her reflection, she breathes the name and clouds the shaving-glass.

MRS BEYNON (*Loudly, from above*)

Lily!

LILY SMALLS (*Loudly*)

Yes, mum.

MRS BEYNON

Where's my tea, girl?

LILY SMALLS

(*Softly*) Where d'you think? In the cat-box?
(*Loudly*) Coming up, mum.

FIRST VOICE

Mr Pugh, in the School House opposite, takes up the morning tea to Mrs Pugh, and whispers on the stairs

MR PUGH

Here's your arsenic, dear.
And your weedkiller biscuit.
I've throttled your parakeet.
I've spat in the vases.
I've put cheese in the mouseholes.
Here's your . . .   [*Door creaks open*
        . . . nice tea, dear.

MRS PUGH

Too much sugar.

MR PUGH

You haven't tasted it yet, dear.

MRS PUGH

Too much milk, then. Has Mr Jenkins said his poetry?

MR PUGH

Yes, dear.

MRS PUGH

Then it's time to get up.   Give me my glasses.
No, not my *reading* glasses, I want to look *out*.   I want to see

SECOND VOICE

Lily Smalls the treasure down on her red knees washing the front step.

MRS PUGH

She's tucked her dress in her bloomers—oh, the baggage!

SECOND VOICE

P.C. Attila Rees, ox-broad, barge-booted, stamping out of Handcuff House in a heavy beef-red huff, black-browed under his damp helmet . . .

MRS PUGH

He's going to arrest Polly Garter, mark my words.

MR PUGH

What for, dear?

MRS PUGH

For having babies.

28

. . . and lumbering down towards the strand to see that the sea is still there.

FIRST VOICE
Mary Ann Sailors, opening her bedroom window above the taproom and calling out to the heavens

MARY ANN SAILORS
I'm eighty-five years three months and a day!

MRS PUGH
I will say this for her, she never makes a mistake.

FIRST VOICE
Organ Morgan at his bedroom window playing chords on the sill to the morning fishwife gulls who, heckling over Donkey Street, observe

DAI BREAD
Me, Dai Bread, hurrying to the bakery, pushing in my shirt-tails, buttoning my waistcoat, ping goes a button, why can't they sew them, no time for breakfast, nothing for breakfast, there's wives for you.

MRS DAI BREAD ONE
Me, Mrs Dai Bread One, capped and shawled and no old corset, nice to be comfy, nice to be nice, clogging on the cobbles to stir up a neighbour. Oh, Mrs Sarah, can you spare a loaf, love? Dai Bread forgot the bread. There's a lovely morning! How's your boils this morning? Isn't that good news now, it's a change to sit down. Ta, Mrs Sarah.

Me, Mrs Dai Bread Two, gypsied to kill in a silky scarlet petticoat above my knees, dirty pretty knees, see my body through my petticoat brown as a berry, high-heel shoes with one heel missing, tortoiseshell comb in my bright black slinky hair, nothing else at all but a dab of scent, lolling gaudy at the doorway, tell your fortune in the tea-leaves, scowling at the sunshine, lighting up my pipe.

LORD CUT-GLASS

Me, Lord Cut-Glass, in an old frock-coat belonged to Eli Jenkins and a pair of postman's trousers from Bethesda Jumble, running out of doors to empty slops—mind there, Rover!—and then running in again, tick tock.

NOGOOD BOYO

Me, Nogood Boyo, up to no good in the wash-house.

MISS PRICE

Me, Miss Price, in my pretty print housecoat, deft at the clothesline, natty as a jenny-wren, then pit-pat back to my egg in its cosy, my crisp toast-fingers, my home-made plum and butterpat.

POLLY GARTER

Me, Polly Garter, under the washing line, giving the breast in the garden to my bonny new baby. Nothing grows in our garden, only washing. And babies. And where's their fathers live, my love? Over the hills and far away. You're looking up at me now. I know what you're thinking, you poor little milky creature. You're thinking, you're no better than you

should be, Polly, and that's good enough for me.
Oh, isn't life a terrible thing, thank God?

[*Single long high chord on strings*

FIRST VOICE

Now frying-pans spit, kettles and cats purr in the
kitchen. The town smells of seaweed and breakfast
all the way down from Bay View, where Mrs Ogmore-
Pritchard, in smock and turban, big-besomed to engage
the dust, picks at her starchless bread and sips lemon-
rind tea, to Bottom Cottage, where Mr Waldo, in
bowler and bib, gobbles his bubble-and-squeak and
kippers and swigs from the saucebottle. Mary Ann
Sailors

MARY ANN SAILORS

praises the Lord who made porridge.

FIRST VOICE

Mr Pugh

MR PUGH

remembers ground glass as he juggles his omelet.

FIRST VOICE

Mrs Pugh

MRS PUGH

nags the salt-cellar.

FIRST VOICE

Willy Nilly postman

WILLY NILLY

downs his last bucket of black brackish tea and rumbles
out bandy to the clucking back where the hens twitch
and grieve for their tea-soaked sops.

Mrs Willy Nilly

full of tea to her double-chinned brim broods and bubbles over her coven of kettles on the hissing hot range always ready to steam open the mail.

FIRST VOICE
The Reverend Eli Jenkins

REV. ELI JENKINS
finds a rhyme and dips his pen in his cocoa.

FIRST VOICE
Lord Cut-Glass in his ticking kitchen

LORD CUT-GLASS
scampers from clock to clock, a bunch of clock-keys in one hand, a fish-head in the other.

FIRST VOICE
Captain Cat in his galley

CAPTAIN CAT
blind and fine-fingered savours his sea-fry.

FIRST VOICE
Mr and Mrs Cherry Owen, in their Donkey Street room that is bedroom, parlour, kitchen, and scullery, sit down to last night's supper of onions boiled in their overcoats and broth of spuds and baconrind and leeks and bones.

MRS CHERRY OWEN
See that smudge on the wall by the picture of Auntie Blossom?   That's where you threw the sago.

[*Cherry Owen laughs with delight*

32

MRS CHERRY OWEN
You only missed me by a inch.

CHERRY OWEN
I always miss Auntie Blossom too.

MRS CHERRY OWEN
Remember last night? In you reeled, my boy, as drunk as a deacon with a big wet bucket and a fish-frail full of stout and you looked at me and you said, 'God has come home!' you said, and then over the bucket you went, sprawling and bawling, and the floor was all flagons and eels.

CHERRY OWEN
Was I wounded?

MRS CHERRY OWEN
And then you took off your trousers and you said, 'Does anybody want a fight!' Oh, you old baboon.

CHERRY OWEN
Give me a kiss.

MRS CHERRY OWEN
And then you sang 'Bread of Heaven,' tenor and bass.

CHERRY OWEN
I *always* sing 'Bread of Heaven.'

MRS CHERRY OWEN
And then you did a little dance on the table.

CHERRY OWEN
I did?

MRS CHERRY OWEN
Drop dead!

CHERRY OWEN

And then what did I do?

MRS CHERRY OWEN

Then you cried like a baby and said you were a poor drunk orphan with nowhere to go but the grave.

CHERRY OWEN

And what did I do next, my dear?

MRS CHERRY OWEN

Then you danced on the table all over again and said you were King Solomon Owen and I was your Mrs Sheba.

CHERRY OWEN (*Softly*)

And then?

MRS CHERRY OWEN

And then I got you into bed and you snored all night like a brewery.

[*Mr and Mrs Cherry Owen laugh delightedly together*

FIRST VOICE

From Beynon Butchers in Coronation Street, the smell of fried liver sidles out with onions on its breath. And listen! In the dark breakfast-room behind the shop, Mr and Mrs Beynon, waited upon by their treasure, enjoy, between bites, their everymorning hullabaloo, and Mrs Beynon slips the gristly bits under the tasselled tablecloth to her fat cat.

[*Cat purrs*

MRS BEYNON

She likes the liver, Ben.

MR BEYNON

She ought to do, Bess.   It's her brother's.

MRS BEYNON (*Screaming*)

Oh, d'you hear that, Lily?

LILY SMALLS

Yes, mum.

MRS BEYNON

We're eating pusscat.

LILY SMALLS

Yes, mum.

MRS BEYNON

Oh, you cat-butcher!

MR BEYNON

It was doctored, mind.

MRS BEYNON (*Hysterical*)

What's that got to do with it?

MR BEYNON

Yesterday we had mole.

MRS BEYNON

Oh, Lily, Lily!

MR BEYNON

Monday, otter.   Tuesday, shrews.

[*Mrs Beynon screams*

LILY SMALLS

Go on, Mrs Beynon.   He's the biggest liar in town.

MRS BEYNON

Don't you dare say that about Mr Beynon.

35

LILY SMALLS
Everybody knows it, mum.

MRS BEYNON
Mr Beynon never tells a lie.   Do you, Ben?

MR BEYNON
No, Bess.   And now I am going out after the corgies, with my little cleaver.

MRS BEYNON
Oh, Lily, Lily!

FIRST VOICE
Up the street, in the Sailors Arms, Sinbad Sailors, grandson of Mary Ann Sailors, draws a pint in the sunlit bar.   The ship's clock in the bar says half past eleven.   Half past eleven is opening time.   The hands of the clock have stayed still at half past eleven for fifty years.   It is always opening time in the Sailors Arms.

SINBAD
Here's to me, Sinbad.

FIRST VOICE
All over the town, babies and old men are cleaned and put into their broken prams and wheeled on to the sunlit cockled cobbles or out into the backyards under the dancing underclothes, and left.   A baby cries.

OLD MAN
I want my pipe and he wants his bottle.

[*School bell rings*

Noses are wiped, heads picked, hair combed, paws scrubbed, ears boxed, and the children shrilled off to school.

SECOND VOICE

Fishermen grumble to their nets. Nogood Boyo goes out in the dinghy *Zanzibar*, ships the oars, drifts slowly in the dab-filled bay, and, lying on his back in the unbaled water, among crabs' legs and tangled lines, looks up at the spring sky.

NOGOOD BOYO (*Softly, lazily*)

I don't know who's up there and I don't care.

FIRST VOICE

He turns his head and looks up at Llaregyb Hill, and sees, among green lathered trees, the white houses of the strewn away farms, where farmboys whistle, dogs shout, cows low, but all too far away for him, or you, to hear. And in the town, the shops squeak open. Mr Edwards, in butterfly-collar and straw-hat at the doorway of Manchester House, measures with his eye the dawdlers-by for striped flannel shirts and shrouds and flowery blouses, and bellows to himself in the darkness behind his eye

MR EDWARDS (*Whispers*)

I love Miss Price.

FIRST VOICE

Syrup is sold in the post-office. A car drives to

market, full of fowls and a farmer. Milk-churns stand at Coronation Corner like short silver police-men. And, sitting at the open window of Schooner House, blind Captain Cat hears all the morning of the town.

[School bell in background. Children's voices. The noise of children's feet on the cobbles

CAPTAIN CAT *(Softly, to himself)*
Maggie Richards, Ricky Rhys, Tommy Powell, our Sal, little Gerwain, Billy Swansea with the dog's voice, one of Mr Waldo's, nasty Humphrey, Jackie with the sniff. . . . Where's Dicky's Albie? and the boys from Ty-pant? Perhaps they got the rash again.

[A sudden cry among the children's voices

CAPTAIN CAT
Somebody's hit Maggie Richards. Two to one it's Billy Swansea. Never trust a boy who barks.

[A burst of yelping crying
Right again! It's Billy.

FIRST VOICE
And the children's voices cry away.

[Postman's rat-a-tat on door, distant

CAPTAIN CAT *(Softly, to himself)*
That's Willy Nilly knocking at Bay View. Rat-a-tat, very soft. The knocker's got a kid glove on. Who's sent a letter to Mrs Ogmore-Pritchard?

[Rat-a-tat, distant again

Careful now, she swabs the front glassy. Every step's like a bar of soap. Mind your size twelveses. That old Bessie would beeswax the lawn to make the birds slip.

WILLY NILLY

Morning, Mrs Ogmore-Pritchard.

MRS OGMORE-PRITCHARD

Good morning, postman.

WILLY NILLY

Here's a letter for you with stamped and addressed envelope enclosed, all the way from Builth Wells. A gentleman wants to study birds and can he have accommodation for two weeks and a bath vegetarian.

MRS OGMORE-PRITCHARD

No.

WILLY NILLY (*Persuasively*)

You wouldn't know he was in the house, Mrs Ogmore-Pritchard. He'd be out in the mornings at the bang of dawn with his bag of breadcrumbs and his little telescope . . .

MRS OGMORE-PRITCHARD

And come home at all hours covered with feathers. I don't want persons in my nice clean rooms breathing all over the chairs . . .

WILLY NILLY

Cross my heart, he won't breathe.

. . . and putting their feet on my carpets and sneezing on my china and sleeping in my sheets . . .

WILLY NILLY

He only wants a *single* bed, Mrs Ogmore-Pritchard.

[*Door slams*

CAPTAIN CAT (*Softly*)

And back she goes to the kitchen to polish the potatoes.

FIRST VOICE

Captain Cat hears Willy Nilly's feet heavy on the distant cobbles.

CAPTAIN CAT

One, two, three, four, five. . . . That's Mrs Rose Cottage. What's to-day? To-day she gets the letter from her sister in Gorslas. How's the twins' teeth?

He's stopping at School House.

WILLY NILLY

Morning, Mrs Pugh. Mrs Ogmore-Pritchard won't have a gentleman in from Builth Wells because he'll sleep in her sheets, Mrs Rose Cottage's sister in Gorslas's twins have got to have them out . . .

MRS PUGH

Give me the parcel.

WILLY NILLY

It's for *Mr* Pugh, Mrs Pugh.

MRS PUGH

Never you mind. What's inside it?

A book called *Lives of the Great Poisoners.*

CAPTAIN CAT
That's Manchester House.

WILLY NILLY
Morning, Mr Edwards. Very small news. Mrs Ogmore-Pritchard won't have birds in the house, and Mr Pugh's bought a book now on how to do in Mrs Pugh.

MR EDWARDS
Have you got a letter from *her*?

WILLY NILLY
Miss Price loves you with all her heart. Smelling of lavender to-day. She's down to the last of the elderflower wine but the quince jam's bearing up and she's knitting roses on the doilies. Last week she sold three jars of boiled sweets, pound of humbugs, half a box of jellybabies and six coloured photos of Llaregyb. Yours for ever. Then twenty-one X's.

MR EDWARDS
Oh, Willy Nilly, she's a ruby! Here's my letter. Put it into her hands now.

[*Slow feet on cobbles, quicker feet approaching*

CAPTAIN CAT
Mr Waldo hurrying to the Sailors Arms. Pint of stout with a egg in it. [*Footsteps stop*

(*Softly*) There's a letter for him.

It's another paternity summons, Mr Waldo.

FIRST VOICE

The quick footsteps hurry on along the cobbles
and up three steps to the Sailors Arms.

MR WALDO (*Calling out*)

Quick, Sinbad. Pint of stout. And no egg in.

FIRST VOICE

People are moving now up and down the cobbled
street.

CAPTAIN CAT

All the women are out this morning, in the sun.
You can tell it's Spring. There goes Mrs Cherry, you
can tell her by her trotters, off she trots new as a
daisy. Who's that talking by the pump? Mrs Floyd
and Boyo, talking flatfish. What can you talk about
flatfish? That's Mrs Dai Bread One, waltzing up the
street like a jelly, every time she shakes it's slap slap
slap. Who's that? Mrs Butcher Beynon with her
pet black cat, it follows her everywhere, miaow and
all. There goes Mrs Twenty-Three, important, the
sun gets up and goes down in her dewlap, when she
shuts her eyes, it's night. High heels now, in the
morning too, Mrs Rose Cottage's eldest Mae, seventeen
and never been kissed ho ho, going young and milking
under my window to the field with the nannygoats, she
reminds me all the way. Can't hear what the women
are gabbing round the pump. Same as ever. Who's
having a baby, who blacked whose eye, seen Polly
Garter giving her belly an airing, there should be a

42

law, seen Mrs Beynon's new mauve jumper, it's her old grey jumper dyed, who's dead, who's dying, there's a lovely day, oh the cost of soapflakes!

[*Organ music, distant*

CAPTAIN CAT

Organ Morgan's at it early. You can tell it's Spring.

FIRST VOICE

And he hears the noise of milk-cans.

CAPTAIN CAT

Ocky Milkman on his round. I will say this, his milk's as fresh as the dew. Half dew it is. Snuffle on, Ocky, watering the town . . . Somebody's coming. Now the voices round the pump can see somebody coming. Hush, there's a hush! You can tell by the noise of the hush, it's Polly Garter. (*Louder*) Hullo, Polly, who's there?

POLLY GARTER (*Off*)

Me, love.

CAPTAIN CAT

That's Polly Garter. (*Softly*) Hullo, Polly my love, can you hear the dumb goose-hiss of the wives as they huddle and peck or flounce at a waddle away? Who cuddled you when? Which of their gandering hubbies moaned in Milk Wood for your naughty mothering arms and body like a wardrobe, love? Scrub the floors of the Welfare Hall for the Mothers' Union Social Dance, you're one mother won't wriggle her roly poly bum or pat her fat little buttery feet in that wedding-ringed holy to-night though the waltzing

43

breadwinners snatched from the cosy smoke of the Sailors Arms will grizzle and mope.

[A cock crows

Too late, cock, too late

for the town's half over with its morning. The morning's busy as bees.

[Organ music fades into silence

There's the clip clop of horses on the sunhoneyed cobbles of the humming streets, hammering of horse-shoes, gobble quack and cackle, tomtit twitter from the bird-ounced boughs, braying on Donkey Down. Bread is baking, pigs are grunting, chop goes the butcher, milk-churns bell, tills ring, sheep cough, dogs shout, saws sing. Oh, the Spring whinny and morning moo from the clog dancing farms, the gulls' gab and rabble on the boat-bobbing river and sea and the cockles bubbling in the sand, scamper of sander-lings, curlew cry, crow caw, pigeon coo, clock strike, bull bellow, and the ragged gabble of the beargarden school as the women scratch and babble in Mrs Organ Morgan's general shop where everything is sold: custard, buckets, henna, rat-traps, shrimp-nets, sugar, stamps, confetti, paraffin, hatchets, whistles.

Mrs Ogmore-Pritchard

la di da

got a man in Builth Wells

and he got a little telescope to look at birds

Willy Nilly said

Remember her first husband? He didn't need a telescope

he looked at them undressing through the keyhole

and he used to shout Tallyho

but Mr Ogmore was a proper gentleman

even though he hanged his collie.

Seen Mrs Butcher Beynon?

she said Butcher Beynon put dogs in the mincer

go on, he's pulling her leg

now don't you dare tell her that, there's a dear

or she'll think he's trying to pull it off and eat it.

FOURTH WOMAN
There's a nasty lot live here when you come to think.

FIRST WOMAN
Look at that Nogood Boyo now

SECOND WOMAN
too lazy to wipe his snout

THIRD WOMAN
and going out fishing every day and all he ever brought back was a Mrs Samuels

FIRST WOMAN
been in the water a week.

SECOND WOMAN
And look at Ocky Milkman's wife that nobody's ever seen

FIRST WOMAN
he keeps her in the cupboard with the empties

THIRD WOMAN
and think of Dai Bread with two wives

SECOND WOMAN
one for the daytime one for the night.

FOURTH WOMAN
Men are brutes on the quiet.

THIRD WOMAN
And how's Organ Morgan, Mrs Morgan?

FIRST WOMAN
you look dead beat

SECOND WOMAN
it's organ organ all the time with him

THIRD WOMAN
up every night until midnight playing the organ.

MRS ORGAN MORGAN
Oh, I'm a martyr to music.

FIRST VOICE
Outside, the sun springs down on the rough and tumbling town. It runs through the hedges of Goosegog Lane, cuffing the birds to sing. Spring whips green down Cockle Row, and the shells ring out. Llaregyb this snip of a morning is wildfruit and warm, the streets, fields, sands and waters springing in the young sun.

SECOND VOICE
Evans the Death presses hard with black gloves on the coffin of his breast in case his heart jumps out.

EVANS THE DEATH (*Harshly*)
Where's your dignity. Lie down.

SECOND VOICE
Spring stirs Gossamer Beynon schoolmistress like a spoon.

GOSSAMER BEYNON (*Tearfully*)
Oh, what can I do? I'll *never* be refined if I twitch.

SECOND VOICE
Spring this strong morning foams in a flame in Jack Black as he cobbles a high-heeled shoe for Mrs Dai Bread Two the gypsy, but he hammers it sternly out.

JACK BLACK (*To a hammer rhythm*)
There is *no leg* belonging to the foot that belongs to
this shoe.

SECOND VOICE
The sun and the green breeze ship Captain Cat
sea-memory again.

CAPTAIN CAT
No, *I'll* take the mulatto, by God, who's captain
here? Parlez-vous jig jig, Madam?

SECOND VOICE
Mary Ann Sailors says very softly to herself as she
looks out at Llaregyb Hill from the bedroom where
she was born

MARY ANN SAILORS (*Loudly*)
It is Spring in Llaregyb in the sun in my old age,
and this is the Chosen Land.
[*A choir of children's voices suddenly cries out on one,*
high, glad, long, sighing note

FIRST VOICE
And in Willy Nilly the Postman's dark and sizzling
damp tea-coated misty pygmy kitchen where the
spittingcat kettles throb and hop on the range, Mrs
Willy Nilly steams open Mr Mog Edwards' letter to
Miss Myfanwy Price and reads it aloud to Willy Nilly
by the squint of the Spring sun through the one sealed
window running with tears, while the drugged, be-
draggled hens at the back door whimper and snivel
for the lickerish bog-black tea.

48

From Manchester House, Llaregyb. Sole Prop: Mr Mog Edwards (late of Twll), Linendraper, Haberdasher, Master Tailor, Costumier. For West End Negligee, Lingerie, Teagowns, Evening Dress, Trousseaux, Layettes. Also Ready to Wear for All Occasions. Economical Outfitting for Agricultural Employment Our Speciality, Wardrobes Bought. Among Our Satisfied Customers Ministers of Religion and J.P's. Fittings by Appointment. Advertising Weekly in the *Twll Bugle*. Beloved Myfanwy Price my Bride in Heaven,

MOG EDWARDS

I love you until Death do us part and then we shall be together for ever and ever. A new parcel of ribbons has come from Carmarthen to-day, all the colours in the rainbow. I wish I could tie a ribbon in your hair a white one but it cannot be. I dreamed last night you were all dripping wet and you sat on my lap as the Reverend Jenkins went down the street. I see you got a mermaid in your lap he said and he lifted his hat. He is a proper Christian. Not like Cherry Owen who said you should have thrown her back he said. Business is very poorly. Polly Garter bought two garters with roses but she never got stockings so what is the use I say. Mr Waldo tried to sell me a woman's nightie outsize he said he found it and we know where. I sold a packet of pins to Tom the Sailors to pick his teeth. If this goes on I shall be in the workhouse. My heart is in your bosom and yours is in mine. God be with you always Myfanwy Price and keep you lovely

49

for me in His Heavenly Mansion. I must stop now and remain, Your Eternal, Mog Edwards.

And then a little message with a rubber stamp. Shop at Mog's!!!

And Willy Nilly, rumbling, jockeys out again to the three-seated shack called the House of Commons in the back where the hens weep, and sees, in sudden Springshine,

herring gulls heckling down to the harbour where the fishermen spit and prop the morning up and eye the fishy sea smooth to the sea's end as it lulls in blue. Green and gold money, tobacco, tinned salmon, hats with feathers, pots of fish-paste, warmth for the winter-to-be, weave and leap in it rich and slippery in the flash and shapes of fishes through the cold sea-streets. But with blue lazy eyes the fishermen gaze at that milkmaid whispering water with no ruck or ripple as though it blew great guns and serpents and typhooned the town.

Too rough for fishing to-day.

And they thank God, and gob at a gull for luck, and moss-slow and silent make their way uphill, from the still still sea, towards the Sailors Arms as the children

[School bell

spank and scamper rough and singing out of school
into the draggletail yard. And Captain Cat at his
window says soft to himself the words of their song.

CAPTAIN CAT (*To the beat of the singing*)
Johnnie Crack and Flossie Snail
Kept their baby in a milking pail
Flossie Snail and Johnnie Crack
One would pull it out and one would put it back

O it's my turn now said Flossie Snail
To take the baby from the milking pail
And it's my turn now said Johnnie Crack
To smack it on the head and put it back

Johnnie Crack and Flossie Snail
Kept their baby in a milking pail
One would put it back and one would pull it out
And all it had to drink was ale and stout
For Johnnie Crack and Flossie Snail
Always used to say that stout and ale
Was *good* for a baby in a milking pail.

[*Long pause*

FIRST VOICE

The music of the spheres is heard distinctly over
Milk Wood. It is 'The Rustle of Spring.'

SECOND VOICE

A glee-party sings in Bethesda Graveyard, gay but
muffled.

FIRST VOICE

Vegetables make love above the tenors

51

and dogs bark blue in the face.

Mrs Ogmore-Pritchard belches in a teeny hanky
and chases the sunlight with a flywhisk, but even she
cannot drive out the Spring: from one of the finger-
bowls a primrose grows.

Mrs Dai Bread One and Mrs Dai Bread Two are
sitting outside their house in Donkey Lane, one darkly
one plumply blooming in the quick, dewy sun. Mrs
Dai Bread Two is looking into a crystal ball which she
holds in the lap of her dirty yellow petticoat, hard
against her hard dark thighs.

MRS DAI BREAD TWO
Cross my palm with silver. Out of our housekeeping
money. Aah!

MRS DAI BREAD ONE
What d'you see, lovie?

MRS DAI BREAD TWO
I see a featherbed. With three pillows on it.
And a text above the bed. I can't read what it says,
there's great clouds blowing. Now they have blown
away. God is Love, the text says.

MRS DAI BREAD ONE (*Delighted*)
That's *our* bed.

MRS DAI BREAD TWO
And now it's vanished. The sun's spinning like a
top. Who's this coming out of the sun? It's a
hairy little man with big pink lips. He got a wall eye.

MRS DAI BREAD ONE
It's Dai, it's Dai Bread!

MRS DAI BREAD TWO
Ssh! The featherbed's floating back. The little man's taking his boots off. He's pulling his shirt over his head. He's beating his chest with his fists. He's climbing into bed.

MRS DAI BREAD ONE
Go on, go on.

MRS DAI BREAD TWO
There's *two* women in bed. He looks at them both, with his head cocked on one side. He's whistling through his teeth. Now he grips his little arms round one of the women.

MRS DAI BREAD ONE
Which one, which one?

MRS DAI BREAD TWO
I can't see any more. There's great clouds blowing again.

MRS DAI BREAD ONE
Ach, the mean old clouds!
> [*Pause. The children's singing fades*

FIRST VOICE
The morning is all singing. The Reverend Eli Jenkins, busy on his morning calls, stops outside the Welfare Hall to hear Polly Garter as she scrubs the floors for the Mothers' Union Dance to-night.

POLLY GARTER (*Singing*)

I loved a man whose name was Tom
He was strong as a bear and two yards long
I loved a man whose name was Dick
He was big as a barrel and three feet thick
And I loved a man whose name was Harry
Six feet tall and sweet as a cherry
But the one I loved best awake or asleep
Was little Willy Wee and he's six feet deep.

O Tom Dick and Harry were three fine men
And I'll never have such loving again
But little Willy Wee who took me on his knee
Little Willy Wee was the man for me.

Now men from every parish round
Run after me and roll me on the ground
But whenever I love another man back
Johnnie from the Hill or Sailing Jack
I always think as they do what they please
Of Tom Dick and Harry who were tall as trees
And most I think when I'm by their side
Of little Willy Wee who downed and died.

O Tom Dick and Harry were three fine men
And I'll never have such loving again
But little Willy Wee who took me on his knee
Little Willy Weazel is the man for me.

REV. ELI JENKINS

Praise the Lord!   We are a musical nation.

SECOND VOICE

And the Reverend Jenkins hurries on through the
town to visit the sick with jelly and poems.

FIRST VOICE
The town's as full as a lovebird's egg.

MR WALDO
There goes the Reverend,

FIRST VOICE
says Mr Waldo at the smoked herring brown window of the unwashed Sailors Arms,

MR WALDO
with his brolly and his odes. Fill 'em up, Sinbad, I'm on the treacle to-day.

SECOND VOICE
The silent fishermen flush down their pints.

SINBAD
Oh, Mr Waldo,

FIRST VOICE
sighs Sinbad Sailors,

SINBAD
I dote on that Gossamer Beynon. She's a lady all over.

FIRST VOICE
And Mr Waldo, who is thinking of a woman soft as Eve and sharp as sciatica to share his bread-pudding bed, answers

MR WALDO
No lady that I know is.

SINBAD
And if only grandma'd die, cross my heart I'd go down on my knees Mr Waldo and I'd say Miss Gossamer I'd say

E

55

CHILDREN'S VOICES

When birds do sing hey ding a ding a ding
Sweet lovers love the Spring . . .

SECOND VOICE

Polly Garter sings, still on her knees,

POLLY GARTER

Tom Dick and Harry were three fine men
And I'll never have such

CHILDREN

ding a ding

POLLY GARTER

again.

FIRST VOICE

And the morning school is over, and Captain Cat at his curtained schooner's porthole open to the Spring sun tides hears the naughty forfeiting children tumble and rhyme on the cobbles.

GIRLS' VOICES

Gwennie call the boys
They make such a noise.

GIRL

Boys boys boys
Come along to me.

GIRLS' VOICES

Boys boys boys
Kiss Gwennie where she says
Or give her a penny.
Go on, Gwennie.

Kiss me in Goosegog Lane
Or give me a penny.
What's your name?

FIRST BOY

Billy.

GIRL

Kiss me in Goosegog Lane Billy
Or give me a penny silly.

FIRST BOY

Gwennie Gwennie
I kiss you in Goosegog Lane.
Now I haven't got to give you a penny.

GIRLS' VOICES

Boys boys boys
Kiss Gwennie where she says
Or give her a penny.
Go on, Gwennie.

GIRL

Kiss me on Llaregyb Hill
Or give me a penny.
What's your name?

SECOND BOY

Johnnie Cristo.

GIRL

Kiss me on Llaregyb Hill Johnnie Cristo
Or give me a penny mister.

SECOND BOY

Gwennie Gwennie
I kiss you on Llaregyb Hill.
Now I haven't got to give you a penny.

GIRLS' VOICES

Boys boys boys
Kiss Gwennie where she says
Or give her a penny.
Go on, Gwennie.

GIRL

Kiss me in Milk Wood
Or give me a penny.
What's your name?

THIRD BOY

Dicky.

GIRL

Kiss me in Milk Wood Dicky
Or give me a penny quickly.

THIRD BOY

Gwennie Gwennie
I can't kiss you in Milk Wood.

GIRLS' VOICES

Gwennie ask him why.

GIRL

Why?

Because my mother says I mustn't.

Cowardy cowardy custard
Give Gwennie a penny.

Give me a penny.

I haven't got any.

Put him in the river
Up to his liver
Quick quick Dirty Dick
Beat him on the bum
With a rhubarb stick.
Aiee!
Hush!

And the shrill girls giggle and master around him
and squeal as they clutch and thrash, and he blubbers
away downhill with his patched pants falling, and his
tear-splashed blush burns all the way as the triumphant
bird-like sisters scream with buttons in their claws
and the bully brothers hoot after him his little nickname
and his mother's shame and his father's wickedness
with the loose wild barefoot women of the hovels of
the hills. It all means nothing at all, and, howling
for his milky mum, for her cawl and buttermilk and
cowbreath and welshcakes and the fat birth-smelling

bed and moonlit kitchen of her arms, he'll never forget as he paddles blind home through the weeping end of the world. Then his tormentors tussle and run to the Cockle Street sweet-shop, their pennies sticky as honey, to buy from Miss Myfanwy Price, who is cocky and neat as a puff-bosomed robin and her small round buttocks tight as ticks, gobstoppers big as wens that rainbow as you suck, brandyballs, winegums, hundreds and thousands, liquorice sweet as sick, nougat to tug and ribbon out like another red rubbery tongue, gum to glue in girls' curls, crimson coughdrops to spit blood, ice-cream cornets, dandelion-and-burdock, raspberry and cherryade, pop goes the weasel and the wind.

SECOND VOICE

Gossamer Beynon high-heels out of school. The sun hums down through the cotton flowers of her dress into the bell of her heart and buzzes in the honey there and couches and kisses, lazy-loving and boozed, in her red-berried breast. Eyes run from the trees and windows of the street, steaming 'Gossamer,' and strip her to the nipples and the bees. She blazes naked past the Sailors Arms, the only woman on the Dai-Adamed earth. Sinbad Sailors places on her thighs still dewdamp from the first mangrowing cock-crow garden his reverent goat-bearded hands.

GOSSAMER BEYNON

I don't care if he *is* common,

SECOND VOICE

she whispers to her salad-day deep self,

60

I want to gobble him up.   I don't care if he *does* drop his aitches,

SECOND VOICE

she tells the stripped and mother-of-the-world big-beamed and Eve-hipped spring of her self,

GOSSAMER BEYNON

so long as he's all cucumber and hooves.

SECOND VOICE

Sinbad Sailors watches her go by, demure and proud and schoolmarm in her crisp flower dress and sun-defying hat, with never a look or lilt or wriggle, the butcher's unmelting icemaiden daughter veiled for ever from the hungry hug of his eyes.

SINBAD SAILORS

Oh, Gossamer Beynon, why are you so proud?

SECOND VOICE

he grieves to his guinness,

SINBAD SAILORS

Oh, beautiful beautiful Gossamer B, I wish I wish that you were for me.   I wish you were not so edu-cated.

SECOND VOICE

She feels his goatbeard tickle her in the middle of the world like a tuft of wiry fire, and she turns in a terror of delight away from his whips and whiskery conflagration, and sits down in the kitchen to a plate heaped high with chips and the kidneys of lambs.

In the blind-drawn dark dining-room of School
House, dusty and echoing as a dining-room in a vault,
Mr and Mrs Pugh are silent over cold grey cottage pie.
Mr Pugh reads, as he forks the shroud meat in, from
Lives of the Great Poisoners. He has bound a plain
brown-paper cover round the book. Slyly, between
slow mouthfuls, he sidespies up at Mrs Pugh, poisons
her with his eye, then goes on reading. He under-
lines certain passages and smiles in secret.

MRS PUGH

Persons with manners do not read at table,

FIRST VOICE

says Mrs Pugh. She swallows a digestive tablet as big
as a horse-pill, washing it down with clouded peasoup
water.

[Pause

MRS PUGH

Some persons were brought up in pigsties.

MR PUGH

Pigs don't read at table, dear.

FIRST VOICE

Bitterly she flicks dust from the broken cruet.
It settles on the pie in a thin gnat-rain.

MR PUGH

Pigs can't read, my dear.

MRS PUGH

I know one who can.

Alone in the hissing laboratory of his wishes, Mr Pugh minces among bad vats and jeroboams, tiptoes through spinneys of murdering herbs, agony dancing in his crucibles, and mixes especially for Mrs Pugh a venomous porridge unknown to toxicologists which will scald and viper through her until her ears fall off like figs, her toes grow big and black as balloons, and steam comes screaming out of her navel.

MR PUGH

You know best, dear,

FIRST VOICE

says Mr Pugh, and quick as a flash he ducks her in rat soup.

MRS PUGH

What's that book by your trough, Mr Pugh?

MR PUGH

It's a theological work, my dear. *Lives of the Great Saints.*

FIRST VOICE

Mrs Pugh smiles. An icicle forms in the cold air of the dining-vault.

MRS PUGH

I saw you talking to a saint this morning. Saint Polly Garter. She was martyred again last night. Mrs Organ Morgan saw her with Mr Waldo.

MRS ORGAN MORGAN

And when they saw me they pretended they were looking for nests, said Mrs Organ Morgan to her husband, with her mouth full of fish as a pelican's.

MRS ORGAN MORGAN

But you don't go nesting in long combinations, I said to myself, like Mr Waldo was wearing, and your dress nearly over your head like Polly Garter's. Oh, they didn't fool me.

SECOND VOICE

One big bird gulp, and the flounder's gone. She licks her lips and goes stabbing again.

MRS ORGAN MORGAN

And when you think of all those babies she's got, then all I can say is she'd better give up bird nesting that's all I can say, it isn't the right kind of hobby at all for a woman that can't say No even to midgets. Remember Bob Spit? He wasn't any bigger than a baby and he gave her two. But they're two nice boys, I will say that, Fred Spit and Arthur. Sometimes I like Fred best and sometimes I like Arthur. Who do you like best, Organ?

ORGAN MORGAN

Oh, Bach without any doubt. Bach every time for me.

MRS ORGAN MORGAN

Organ Morgan, you haven't been listening to a word I said. It's organ organ all the time with you . . .

And she bursts into tears, and, in the middle of her salty howling, nimbly spears a small flatfish and pelicans it whole.

ORGAN MORGAN

And then Palestrina,

SECOND VOICE

says Organ Morgan.

FIRST VOICE

Lord Cut-Glass, in his kitchen full of time, squats down alone to a dogdish, marked Fido, of peppery fish-scraps and listens to the voices of his sixty-six clocks, one for each year of his loony age, and watches, with love, their black-and-white moony loudlipped faces tocking the earth away: slow clocks, quick clocks, pendulumed heart-knocks, china, alarm, grandfather, cuckoo; clocks shaped like Noah's whirring Ark, clocks that bicker in marble ships, clocks in the wombs of glass women, hourglass chimers, tu-wit-tu-woo clocks, clocks that pluck tunes, Vesuvius clocks all black bells and lava, Niagara clocks that cataract their ticks, old time-weeping clocks with ebony beards, clocks with no hands for ever drumming out time without ever knowing what time it is. His sixty-six singers are all set at different hours. Lord Cut-Glass lives in a house and a life at siege. Any minute or dark day now, the unknown enemy will loot and savage downhill, but they will not catch him napping. Sixty-six different times in his fish-slimy kitchen ping, strike, tick, chime, and tock.

The lust and lilt and lather and emerald breeze and crackle of the bird-praise and body of Spring with its breasts full of rivering May-milk, means, to that lordly fish-head nibbler, nothing but another nearness to the tribes and navies of the Last Black Day who'll sear and pillage down Armageddon Hill to his double-locked rusty-shuttered tick-tock dust-scrabbled shack at the bottom of the town that has fallen head over bells in love.

POLLY GARTER

And I'll never have such loving again,

SECOND VOICE

pretty Polly hums and longs.

POLLY GARTER (*Sings*)

Now when farmers' boys on the first fair day
Come down from the hills to drink and be gay,
Before the sun sinks I'll lie there in their arms
For they're *good* bad boys from the lonely farms,

But I always think as we tumble into bed
Of little Willy Wee who is dead, dead, dead. . . .

[*A silence*

FIRST VOICE

The sunny slow lulling afternoon yawns and moons through the dozy town. The sea lolls, laps and idles in, with fishes sleeping in its lap. The meadows still as Sunday, the shut-eye tasselled bulls, the goat-and-daisy dingles, nap happy and lazy. The dumb duck-

66

ponds snooze. Clouds sag and pillow on Llaregyb Hill. Pigs grunt in a wet wallow-bath, and smile as they snort and dream. They dream of the acorned swill of the world, the rooting for pig-fruit, the bag-pipe dugs of the mother sow, the squeal and snuffle of yesses of the women pigs in rut. They mud-bask and snout in the pig-loving sun; their tails curl; they rollick and slobber and snore to deep, smug, after-swill sleep. Donkeys angelically drowse on Donkey Down.

MRS PUGH

Persons with manners,

SECOND VOICE

snaps Mrs cold Pugh,

MRS PUGH

do not nod at table.

FIRST VOICE

Mr Pugh cringes awake. He puts on a soft-soaping smile: it is sad and grey under his nicotine-eggyellow weeping walrus Victorian moustache worn thick and long in memory of Doctor Crippen.

MRS PUGH

You should wait until you retire to your sty,

SECOND VOICE

says Mrs Pugh, sweet as a razor. His fawning measly quarter-smile freezes. Sly and silent, he foxes into his chemist's den and there, in a hiss and prussic circle

67

of cauldrons and phials brimful with pox and the Black Death, cooks up a fricassee of deadly night-shade, nicotine, hot frog, cyanide and bat-spit for his needling stalactite hag and bednag of a pokerbacked nutcracker wife.

I beg your pardon, my dear,

he murmurs with a wheedle.

Captain Cat, at his window thrown wide to the sun and the clippered seas he sailed long ago when his eyes were blue and bright, slumbers and voyages; ear-ringed and rolling, I Love You Rosie Probert tattooed on his belly, he brawls with broken bottles in the fug and babel of the dark dock bars, roves with a herd of short and good time cows in every naughty port and twines and souses with the drowned and blowzy-breasted dead. He weeps as he sleeps and sails.

One voice of all he remembers most dearly as his dream buckets down. Lazy early Rosie with the flaxen thatch, whom he shared with Tom-Fred the donkeyman and many another seaman, clearly and near to him speaks from the bedroom of her dust. In that gulf and haven, fleets by the dozen have anchored for the little heaven of the night; but she speaks to Captain napping Cat alone. Mrs Probert . . .

from Duck Lane, Jack. Quack twice and ask for Rosie

SECOND VOICE

. . . is the one love of his sea-life that was sardined with women.

ROSIE PROBERT (*Softly*)

What seas did you see,
Tom Cat, Tom Cat,
In your sailoring days
Long long ago?
What sea beasts were
In the wavery green
When you were my master?

CAPTAIN CAT

I'll tell you the truth.
Seas barking like seals,
Blue seas and green,
Seas covered with eels
And mermen and whales.

ROSIE PROBERT

What seas did you sail
Old whaler when
On the blubbery waves
Between Frisco and Wales
You were my bosun?

CAPTAIN CAT

As true as I'm here
Dear you Tom Cat's tart
You landlubber Rosie

You cosy love
My easy as easy
My true sweetheart,
Seas green as a bean
Seas gliding with swans
In the seal-barking moon.

ROSIE PROBERT

What seas were rocking
My little deck hand
My favourite husband
In your seaboots and hunger
My duck my whaler
My honey my daddy
My pretty sugar sailor
With my name on your belly
When you were a boy
Long long ago?

CAPTAIN CAT

I'll tell you no lies.
The only sea I saw
Was the seesaw sea
With you riding on it.
Lie down, lie easy.
Let me shipwreck in your thighs.

ROSIE PROBERT

Knock twice, Jack,
At the door of my grave
And ask for Rosie.

CAPTAIN CAT

Rosie Probert.

Remember her.
She is forgetting.
The earth which filled her mouth
Is vanishing from her.
Remember me.
I have forgotten you.
I am going into the darkness of the darkness for ever.
I have forgotten that I was ever born.

CHILD

Look,

FIRST VOICE

says a child to her mother as they pass by the window of
Schooner House,

CHILD

Captain Cat is crying

FIRST VOICE

Captain Cat is crying

CAPTAIN CAT

Come back, come back,

FIRST VOICE

up the silences and echoes of the passages of the eternal
night.

CHILD

He's crying all over his nose,

FIRST VOICE

says the child.   Mother and child move on down the
street.

CHILD

He's got a nose like strawberries,

FIRST VOICE

the child says; and then she forgets him too. She sees in the still middle of the bluebagged bay Nogood Boyo fishing from the *Zanzibar*.

CHILD

Nogood Boyo gave me three pennies yesterday but I wouldn't,

FIRST VOICE

the child tells her mother.

SECOND VOICE

Boyo catches a whalebone corset. It is all he has caught all day.

NOGOOD BOYO

Bloody funny fish!

SECOND VOICE

Mrs Dai Bread Two gypsies up his mind's slow eye, dressed only in a bangle.

NOGOOD BOYO

She's wearing her nightgown. (*Pleadingly*) Would you like this nice wet corset, Mrs Dai Bread Two?

MRS DAI BREAD TWO

No, I *won't*!

NOGOOD BOYO

And a bite of my little apple?

he offers with no hope.

She shakes her brass nightgown, and he chases her out of his mind; and when he comes gusting back, there in the bloodshot centre of his eye a geisha girl grins and bows in a kimono of ricepaper.

NOGOOD BOYO

I want to be *good* Boyo, but nobody'll let me,

FIRST VOICE

he sighs as she writhes politely.   The land fades, the sea flocks silently away; and through the warm white cloud where he lies, silky, tingling, uneasy Eastern music undoes him in a Japanese minute.

SECOND VOICE

The afternoon buzzes like lazy bees round the flowers round Mae Rose Cottage.   Nearly asleep in the field of nannygoats who hum and gently butt the sun, she blows love on a puffball.

MAE ROSE COTTAGE (*Lazily*)

He loves me

He loves me not

He loves me

He loves me not

He *loves* me!—the dirty old fool.

SECOND VOICE

Lazy she lies alone in clover and sweet-grass, seventeen and never been sweet in the grass ho ho.

The Reverend Eli Jenkins inky in his cool front parlour or poem-room tells only the truth in his Lifework—the Population, Main Industry, Shipping, History, Topography, Flora and Fauna of the town he worships in—the White Book of Llaregyb. Portraits of famous bards and preachers, all fur and wool from the squint to the kneecaps, hang over him heavy as sheep, next to faint lady watercolours of pale green Milk Wood like a lettuce salad dying. His mother, propped against a pot in a palm, with her wedding-ring waist and bust like a black-clothed dining-table suffers in her stays.

REV. ELI JENKINS

Oh angels be careful there with your knives and forks,

FIRST VOICE

he prays. There is no known likeness of his father Esau, who, undogcollared because of his little weakness, was scythed to the bone one harvest by mistake when sleeping with his weakness in the corn. He lost all ambition and died, with one leg.

REV. ELI JENKINS

Poor Dad,

SECOND VOICE

grieves the Reverend Eli,

REV. ELI JENKINS

to die of drink and agriculture.

Farmer Watkins in Salt Lake Farm hates his cattle
on the hill as he ho's them in to milking.

UTAH WATKINS (*In a fury*)
Damn you, you damned dairies!

SECOND VOICE
A cow kisses him.

UTAH WATKINS
Bite her to death!

SECOND VOICE
he shouts to his deaf dog who smiles and licks his hands.

UTAH WATKINS
Gore him, sit on him, Daisy!

SECOND VOICE
he bawls to the cow who barbed him with her tongue,
and she moos gentle words as he raves and dances
among his summerbreathed slaves walking delicately
to the farm. The coming of the end of the Spring day
is already reflected in the lakes of their great eyes.
Bessie Bighead greets them by the names she gave
them when they were maidens.

BESSIE BIGHEAD
Peg, Meg, Buttercup, Moll,
Fan from the Castle,
Theodosia and Daisy.

SECOND VOICE
They bow their heads.

Look up Bessie Bighead in the White Book of Llaregyb and you will find the few haggard rags and the one
poor glittering thread of her history laid out in pages
there with as much love and care as the lock of hair
of a first lost love. Conceived in Milk Wood, born
in a barn, wrapped in paper, left on a doorstep, big-
headed and bass-voiced she grew in the dark until
long-dead Gomer Owen kissed her when she wasn't
looking because he was dared. Now in the light she'll
work, sing, milk, say the cows' sweet names and sleep
until the night sucks out her soul and spits it into the
sky. In her life-long love light, holily Bessie milks
the fond lake-eyed cows as dusk showers slowly down
over byre, sea and town.

Utah Watkins curses through the farmyard on a
carthorse.

Gallop, you bleeding cripple!

and the huge horse neighs softly as though he had
given it a lump of sugar.

Now the town is dusk. Each cobble, donkey,
goose and gooseberry street is a thoroughfare of dusk;
and dusk and ceremonial dust, and night's first darken-
ing snow, and the sleep of birds, drift under and through
the live dusk of this place of love. Llaregyb is the
capital of dusk.

Mrs Ogmore-Pritchard, at the first drop of the
dusk-shower, seals all her sea-view doors, draws the
germ-free blinds, sits, erect as a dry dream on a high-

backed hygienic chair and wills herself to cold, quick
sleep. At once, at twice, Mr Ogmore and Mr Pritchard, who all dead day long have been gossiping
like ghosts in the woodshed, planning the loveless
destruction of their glass widow, reluctantly sigh and
sidle into her clean house.

MR PRITCHARD

You first, Mr Ogmore.

MR OGMORE

After you, Mr Pritchard.

MR PRITCHARD

No, no, Mr Ogmore. You widowed her first.

FIRST VOICE

And in through the keyhole, with tears where their
eyes once were, they ooze and grumble.

MRS OGMORE-PRITCHARD

Husbands,

FIRST VOICE

she says in her sleep. There is acid love in her voice
for one of the two shambling phantoms. Mr Ogmore
hopes that it is not for him. So does Mr Pritchard.

MRS OGMORE-PRITCHARD

I love you both.

MR OGMORE (*With terror*)

Oh, Mrs Ogmore.

MR PRITCHARD (*With horror*)

Oh, Mrs Pritchard.

MRS OGMORE-PRITCHARD

Soon it will be time to go to bed. Tell me your tasks in order.

MR OGMORE AND MR PRITCHARD

We must take our pyjamas from the drawer marked pyjamas.

MRS OGMORE-PRITCHARD (*Coldly*)

And then you must take them off.

SECOND VOICE

Down in the dusking town, Mae Rose Cottage, still lying in clover, listens to the nannygoats chew, draws circles of lipstick round her nipples.

MAE ROSE COTTAGE

I'm *fast*. I'm a bad lot. God will strike me dead. I'm seventeen. I'll go to hell,

SECOND VOICE

she tells the goats.

MAE ROSE COTTAGE

You just wait. I'll sin till I blow up!

SECOND VOICE

She lies deep, waiting for the worst to happen; the goats champ and sneer.

FIRST VOICE

And at the doorway of Bethesda House, the Reverend Jenkins recites to Llaregyb Hill his sunset poem.

REV. ELI JENKINS

Every morning when I wake,
Dear Lord, a little prayer I make,
O please to keep Thy lovely eye
On all poor creatures born to die.

And every evening at sun-down
I ask a blessing on the town,
For whether we last the night or no
I'm sure is always touch-and-go.

We are not wholly bad or good
Who live our lives under Milk Wood,
And Thou, I know, wilt be the first
To see our best side, not our worst.

O let us see another day!
Bless us this night, I pray,
And to the sun we all will bow
And say, good-bye—but just for now!

FIRST VOICE

Jack Black prepares once more to meet his Satan in
the Wood. He grinds his night-teeth, closes his eyes,
climbs into his religious trousers, their flies sewn up
with cobbler's thread, and pads out, torched and
bibled, grimly, joyfully, into the already sinning dusk.

JACK BLACK

Off to Gomorrah!

SECOND VOICE

And Lily Smalls is up to Nogood Boyo in the wash-
house.

FIRST VOICE

And Cherry Owen, sober as Sunday as he is every day of the week, goes off happy as Saturday to get drunk as a deacon as he does every night.

CHERRY OWEN

I always say she's got two husbands,

FIRST VOICE

says Cherry Owen,

CHERRY OWEN

one drunk and one sober.

FIRST VOICE

And Mrs Cherry simply says

MRS CHERRY OWEN

And aren't I a lucky woman?   Because I love them both.

SINBAD

Evening, Cherry.

CHERRY OWEN

Evening, Sinbad.

SINBAD

What'll you have?

CHERRY OWEN

Too much.

SINBAD

The Sailors Arms is always open . . .

FIRST VOICE

Sinbad suffers to himself, heartbroken,

. . . oh, Gossamer, open yours!

FIRST VOICE

Dusk is drowned for ever until to-morrow. It is all at once night now. The windy town is a hill of windows, and from the larrupped waves the lights of the lamps in the windows call back the day and the dead that have run away to sea. All over the calling dark, babies and old men are bribed and lullabied to sleep.

FIRST WOMAN'S VOICE

Hushabye, baby, the sandman is coming . . .

SECOND WOMAN'S VOICE (*Singing*)

Rockabye, grandpa, in the tree top,
When the wind blows the cradle will rock,
When the bough breaks the cradle will fall,
Down will come grandpa, whiskers and all.

FIRST VOICE

Or their daughters cover up the old unwinking men like parrots, and in their little dark in the lit and bustling young kitchen corners, all night long they watch, beady-eyed, the long night through in case death catches them asleep.

SECOND VOICE

Unmarried girls, alone in their privately bridal bedrooms, powder and curl for the Dance of the World.

[*Accordion music: dim*

They make, in front of their looking-glasses, haughty or come-hithering faces for the young men in the street outside, at the lamplit leaning corners, who wait in the all-at-once wind to wolve and whistle.

[*Accordion music louder, then fading under*

FIRST VOICE
The drinkers in the Sailors Arms drink to the failure of the dance.

A DRINKER
Down with the waltzing and the skipping.

CHERRY OWEN
Dancing isn't natural,

FIRST VOICE
righteously says Cherry Owen who has just downed seventeen pints of flat, warm, thin, Welsh, bitter beer.

SECOND VOICE
A farmer's lantern glimmers, a spark on Llaregyb hillside.

[*Accordion music fades into silence*

FIRST VOICE
Llaregyb Hill, writes the Reverend Jenkins in his poem-room,

REV. ELI JENKINS
Llaregyb Hill, that mystic tumulus, the memorial of peoples that dwelt in the region of Llaregyb before the Celts left the Land of Summer and where the old wizards made themselves a wife out of flowers.

SECOND VOICE
Mr Waldo, in his corner of the Sailors Arms, sings:

In Pembroke City when I was young
I lived by the Castle Keep
Sixpence a week was my wages
For working for the chimbley sweep.
Six cold pennies he gave me
Not a farthing more or less
And all the fare I could afford
Was parsnip gin and watercress.
I did not need a knife and fork
Or a bib up to my chin
To dine on a dish of watercress
And a jug of parsnip gin.
Did you ever hear a growing boy
To live so cruel cheap
On grub that has no flesh and bones
And liquor that makes you weep?
Sweep sweep chimbley sweep,
I wept through Pembroke City
Poor and barefoot in the snow
Till a kind young woman took pity.
Poor little chimbley sweep she said
Black as the ace of spades
O nobody's swept my chimbley
Since my husband went his ways.
Come and sweep my chimbley
Come and sweep my chimbley
She sighed to me with a blush
Come and sweep my chimbley
Come and sweep my chimbley
Bring along your chimbley brush!

Blind Captain Cat climbs into his bunk. Like a cat, he sees in the dark. Through the voyages of his tears he sails to see the dead.

CAPTAIN CAT

Dancing Williams!

FIRST DROWNED

Still dancing.

CAPTAIN CAT

Jonah Jarvis

THIRD DROWNED

Still.

FIRST DROWNED

Curly Bevan's skull.

ROSIE PROBERT

Rosie, with God. She has forgotten dying.

FIRST VOICE

The dead come out in their Sunday best.

SECOND VOICE

Listen to the night breaking.

FIRST VOICE

Organ Morgan goes to chapel to play the organ. He sees Bach lying on a tombstone.

ORGAN MORGAN

Johann Sebastian!

CHERRY OWEN (*Drunkenly*)

Who?

Johann Sebastian mighty Bach.   Oh, Bach fach.

CHERRY OWEN

To hell with you,

FIRST VOICE

says Cherry Owen who is resting on the tombstone on his way home.

Mr Mog Edwards and Miss Myfanwy Price happily apart from one another at the top and the sea end of the town write their everynight letters of love and desire. In the warm White Book of Llaregyb you will find the little maps of the islands of their contentment.

MYFANWY PRICE

Oh, my Mog, I am yours for ever.

FIRST VOICE

And she looks around with pleasure at her own neat neverdull room which Mr Mog Edwards will never enter.

MOG EDWARDS

Come to my arms, Myfanwy.

FIRST VOICE

And he hugs his lovely money to his *own* heart.

And Mr Waldo drunk in the dusky wood hugs his lovely Polly Garter under the eyes and rattling tongues of the neighbours and the birds, and he does not care. He smacks his live red lips.

But it is not *his* name that Polly Garter whispers as she lies under the oak and loves him back.   Six feet deep that name sings in the cold earth.

POLLY GARTER (*Sings*)

But I always think as we tumble into bed
Of little Willy Wee who is dead, dead, dead.

FIRST VOICE

The thin night darkens. A breeze from the creased water sighs the streets close under Milk waking Wood. The Wood, whose every tree-foot's cloven in the black glad sight of the hunters of lovers, that is a God-built garden to Mary Ann Sailors who knows there is Heaven on earth and the chosen people of His kind fire in Llaregyb's land, that is the fairday farmhands' wantoning ignorant chapel of bridesbeds, and, to the Reverend Eli Jenkins, a greenleaved sermon on the innocence of men, the suddenly wind-shaken wood springs awake for the second dark time this one Spring day.

NOTES ON PRONUNCIATION

[Page 2] *Rhiannon*: strongly aspirated *r*, and accent on the second syllable. *Llaregyb*: a voiceless *l* produced from the side of the mouth, accent on the second syllable, the third syllable rhyming with 'bib.' *Dai*: as 'dye.'

[Page 6] *Dowlais*: accent on the first syllable, the second syllable rhyming with 'ice.' *Maesgwyn*: mice-gwin, accent on the second syllable. *Myfanwy*: accent on the second syllable, *f* as *v*, the first *y* an indeterminate sound, the second *y* as *ee*.

[Page 8] *Ach y fi*: the *ch* guttural, the *y* indeterminate, *f* as *v*, the whole pronounced as one word; an interjection expressing disgust.

[Page 12] *mwchins*: a compromise between the English 'mooching' and the Welsh dialect word 'mitching,' playing truant.

[Page 20] *Eisteddfodau*: eye-steth-vod-eye, the *th* voiced, a strong accent on the third syllable. *Parchs*: the *ch* guttural; clergymen.

[Page 21] *Organ Morgan*: the *r*'s rolled, the *o*'s short. *Gippo*: gipsy.

[Page 23] *Dewi*: de-wee; the first syllable, which has the accent, is short.

[Page 24] *Moel yr Wyddfa*: moil-er-ooithva, the *th* voiced. *Carnedd*: the *dd* a voiced *th*, the *r* rolled, accent on the first syllable.

[Page 25] *Penmaenmawr*: 'maen' rhymes with 'line,' 'mawr' with 'hour.' *Sawdde*: southay, the *th* voiced. *Edw*: aid-oo. *Llyfnant*: *y* indeterminate, *f* as v. *Claerwen*,

Cleddau, Dulais: clire-wen; cleth-eye, the *th* voiced; dill-ice.
Ogwr: ogoorr, accent on the first syllable.   *Cennen:* the *c* hard.

[Page 38]   *Gerwain:* gerr-wine, the *g* hard.   *Ty:* as 'tee.'

[Page 40]   *Gorslas:* gorse-lahss, with a strong accent on the second syllable.

[Page 49]   *Twll:* ooll, the *oo* short, the *ll* as in 'Llaregyb.'

[Page 59]   *cawl:* as 'cowl'; a broth with leeks.

[Page 85]   *fach:* an expression of endearment; *f* as *v*, and the *ch* guttural.

FIRST BROADCAST
FULL CAST

First Voice	. . . . .	*Richard Burton*
Second Voice	. . . .	*Richard Bebb*
Captain Cat	. . . . .	*Hugh Griffith*
First Drowned	. . . .	*Dillwyn Owen*
Second Drowned	. . . .	*Meredith Edwards*
Rosie Probert	. . . .	*Rachel Thomas*
Third Drowned	. . . .	*John Huw Jones*
Fourth Drowned	. . . .	*Philip Burton*
Fifth Drowned	. . . .	*John Ormond Thomas*
Mr Mog Edwards	. . . .	*Dafydd Havard*
Miss Myfanwy Price	. . .	*Sybil Williams*
Jack Black	. . . .	*John Glyn Jones*
Waldo's Mother	. . . .	*Olwen Brookes*
Little Boy Waldo	. . . .	*Diana Maddox*
Waldo's Wife	. . . .	*Mary Jones*
Mr Waldo	. . . . .	*Meredith Edwards*
First Neighbour	. . . .	*Dilys Davies*
Second Neighbour	. . . .	*Rachel Roberts*
Third Neighbour	. . . .	*Lorna Davies*
Fourth Neighbour	. . . .	*Gwenllian Owen*
Matti's Mother	. . . .	*Rachel Thomas*
First Woman	. . . .	*Rachel Roberts*
Second Woman	. . . .	*Sybil Williams*
Third Woman	. . . .	*Gwyneth Petty*
Fourth Woman	. . . .	*Olwen Brookes*
Fifth Woman	. . . .	*Lorna Davies*
Preacher	. . . .	*Philip Burton*
Mrs Ogmore-Pritchard	. . .	*Dilys Davies*
Mr Ogmore	. . . .	*David Close-Thomas*
Mr Pritchard	. . . .	*Ben Williams*
Gossamer Beynon	. . . .	*Gwenllian Owen*
Organ Morgan	. . . .	*John Glyn Jones*
Utah Watkins	. . . .	*Meredith Edwards*
Mrs Utah Watkins	. . . .	*Rachel Thomas*

Ocky Milkman	. . . .	*Dillwyn Owen*
A Voice	. . . .	*John Huw Jones*
Mrs Willy Nilly	. . . .	*Rachel Thomas*
Lily Smalls	. . . .	*Gwyneth Petty*
Mae Rose Cottage	. . . .	*Rachel Roberts*
Butcher Beynon	. . . .	*Meredith Edwards*
Rev. Eli Jenkins	. . . .	*Philip Burton*
Mr Pugh	. . . .	*John Huw Jones*
Mrs Organ Morgan	. . . .	*Olwen Brookes*
Mary Ann Sailors	. . . .	*Rachel Thomas*
Dai Bread	. . . .	*David Close-Thomas*
Polly Garter	. . . .	*Diana Maddox*
Nogood Boyo	. . . .	*Dillwyn Owen*
Lord Cut-Glass	. . . .	*John Glyn Jones*
Gwennie	. . . .	*Norma Jones*
Mrs Beynon	. . . .	*Olwen Brookes*
Mrs Pugh	. . . .	*Mary Jones*
Mrs Dai Bread One	. . . .	*Gwyneth Petty*
Mrs Dai Bread Two	. . . .	*Rachel Roberts*
Willy Nilly	. . . .	*Ben Williams*
Mrs Cherry Owen	. . . .	*Lorna Davies*
Cherry Owen	. . . .	*John Ormond Thomas*
Sinbad	. . . .	*Aubrey Richards*
Old Man	. . . .	*David Close-Thomas*
First Neighbour	. . . .	*Gwyneth Petty*
Second Neighbour	. . . .	*Sybil Williams*
Third Neighbour	. . . .	*Lorna Davies*
Fourth Neighbour	. . . .	*Mary Jones*
Evans the Death	. . . .	*Meredith Edwards*
Fisherman	. . . .	*Dillwyn Owen*
Child	. . . .	*Norma Jones*
Bessie Bighead	. . . .	*Gwyneth Petty*
First Woman	. . . .	*Gwenllian Owen*
Second Woman	. . . .	*Rachel Roberts*
A Drinker	. . . .	*Dafydd Havard*

Children of Laugharne School, Carmarthenshire

SONGS

(Music by Daniel Jones)

I. JOHNNIE CRACK AND FLOSSIE SNAIL (page 51)

Childrens' Voices:
Lively

John - nie Crack and Flos - sie Snail kept their ba - by in a milk - ing pail, Flos - sie Snail and John - nie Crack One would pull it out and one would put it back *p Girls:* O it's my turn now said Flos - sie Snail to take the ba - by from the milk - ing pail *p Boys:* And it's my turn now said John - nie Crack to smack it on the head and *All together:* put it back John - nie Crack and Flos - sie Snail kept their ba - by in a milk - ing pail One would put it back and one would pull it out and all it had to drink was ale and stout For John - nie Crack and Flos - sie Snail Al - ways used to say that stout and ale was good for a ba - by in a milk - ing pail.

Moderate speed (= Tempo I)

Girls: Gwen-nie call the boys they make such a noise___ *Gwennie:* Boys boys

Boys Come a long to me *Girls:* Boys Boys Boys kiss Gwen-nie where she

says or give her a pen-ny *Girls speak:-* Go on, Gwennie.

Gwennie: (Slow) Kiss...me... in Goose-gog Lane___ or give me a

pen-ny *Gwennie speaks:-* What's your name? *1st. Boy speaks:* Billy.

Gwennie: (Slow) Kiss...me... in Goose-gog Lane Bil-ly___ *(Tempo I)* or-

give me a pen-ny___ sil-ly *1st Boy (Slow)* Gwen-nie Gwen-nie___ I

(Tempo I) kiss you in Goose-gog Lane *(kiss)* Now I hav-en't got to

give you a pen-ny *Girls: (Tempo I)* Boys Boys Boys kiss Gwen-nie where she

says or give her a pen-ny *Girls speak:-* Go on, Gwennie.

Gwennie: (Slow) Kiss me On Lla-re___gyb Hill *(Tempo I)* Or give me a

pen-ny *Gwennie speaks:-* What's your name?
2nd. Boy speaks: Johnnie Cristo.

Gwennie: (Slow)

Kiss me on Lla-re-gyb Hill John-nie Crist-o

(Tempo I)

Or give me a pen-ny— mis-ter Gwen-nie Gwen-nie—

2nd.Boy (Slow)

(Tempo I)

—— I kiss you on Lla-re-gyb— Hill *(kiss)* Now I

Girls: (Tempo I)

hav-en't got to give you a pen-ny Boys Boys Boys kiss

Girls speak:-
Go on, Gwennie.

Gwen-nie where she says or give her a pen-ny

Gwennie: (Slow) *f* (Tempo I)

Kiss me in Milk Wood or give me a

Gwennie speaks:- What's your name? *3rd. Boy speaks:* Dicky.

pen-ny

Gwennie: (Slow) (Tempo I)

Kiss me in Milk Wood Dic-ky—— Or give me a

3rd.Boy (Slow)

pen-ny— quick-ly Gwen-nie Gwen-nie

3rd. Boy speaks:-
I can't kiss you in Milk Wood.

Girls: (Tempo I)

Gwennie speaks:- Why?
3rd. Boy speaks:-
Because my mother says I mustn't.

Gwen-nie ask him why

Girls: (Fast)

Gwennie:

Cowar-dy Cowar-dy Cus-tard Give Gwennie a pen-ny Give me a

3rd. Boy: *Girls:* (Very fast)

pen-ny I hav-en't got a-ny Put him in the ri-ver

95

Up to his liv - er   Quick quick Dir - ty Dick

Beat him on the bum with a rhu -barb stick Aiee Hush!

Slow (humming) ... Faster

I loved a man whose name was Tom He was strong as a bear and two yards long I loved a man whose name was Dick He was big as a bar-rel and three feet thick And I loved a man whose name was Har-ry Six feet tall and sweet as a cher-ry But the one I loved best a-wake or a-sleep Was Lit-tle Wil-ly Wee and he's six feet deep Oh Tom Dick and Har-ry were three fine men And I'll nev-er have such lo-ving a-gain But Lit-tle Wil-ly Wee who took me on his knee Lit-tle Wil-ly Wee was the man for me Now men from eve-ry pa-rish round Run af-ter me and roll me on the ground But when-e-ver I love a-no-ther man back John-nie from the Hill or Sai-ling Jack I

al____ ways think as they do what they please of
p slower Still slower

Tom Dick and Har -ry who were tall as trees And most I think when I'm
by their side Of Lit - tle Wil - ly Wee who downed and died

f Faster
Oh Tom Dick and Har - ry were three fine men And I'll ne - ver have such
slower *mp* Still slower
lo - ving a - gain But Lit -tle Wil -ly Wee who took me on his knee

p
Lit - tle Wil - ly Wea - zel is the man for__ me
mp (humming)

IV. POLLY GARTER'S SONG (page 56)

Childrens Voices

p
When

Polly Garter

mf Tom Dick and Har - ry were three fine men and I'll

f
birds do sing a ding a ding a ding

ne - ver have such a - gain

98

V. POLLY GARTER'S SONG (page 66)

And I'll ne-ver have such lo-ving a-gain!

Now when far—mers' boys on the first fair day Come down from the hills to drink and be gay Be-fore the sun sinks I'll— Lie there in their arms For they're good bad— boys from the lone-ly farms But I al-ways think as we tum-ble in-to bed Of

Lit-tle Wil-ly Wee——who is dead, dead, dead.

VI. POLLY GARTER'S SONG (page 86)

But I al-ways think as we tum-ble in to bed Of

Lit-tle Wil-ly Wee—— who is dead, dead, dead,

Moderato

In Pem-broke Ci-ty when I was young I lived by the Cast-le Keep_____ Six-pence a week was my wag-es For__wor-king for the chim-bley sweep Six cold pen-nies he gave me Not a far-thing more or less_____ And all the fare I_____ could af-ford was pars-nip gin_____ and __ wa-ter-cress I did not need a knife and fork or a bib up__ to my chin_____ To dine on a dish_____ of wa-ter-cress And a jug of pars-nip gin_____ Did you ev-er hear a grow-ing boy To live so cru-el cheap On grub that has no_____ flesh and bones and liquor that__ makes you weep? Sweep Sweep chim-bley sweep I wept through Pem-broke Ci-ty Poor_____ and bare-foot in the

Slowing down

a Tempo

Slowing down

a Tempo

slower

snow____ Till a kind young wo-man took pi - ty

Poor lit - tle chim - bley sweep____ she said Black as the ace of

spades Oh no - bo - dy's swept____ my chim - bley since my

Slowing down

hus band went____ his ways Come____ and sweep my chim-

With a swing

bley Come____ and sweep my chim - bley she sighed____ to me with a

blush Come____ and sweep my chim - bley Come____ and

sweep my chim - bley Bring a - long your chimbley brush_____